Nation-Building and State Building in Africa

Georges Nzongola-Ntalaja

Occasional Paper Series No. 3

Nation-Building and State Building in Africa

Georges Nzongola-Ntalaja

Nation-Building and State Building in Africa

SAPES BOOKS

HARARE

First published 1993
by SAPES Books
P.O. Box MP 111
Mount Pleasant
Harare
Zimbabwe

© SAPES Trust 1993

Typeset by Southern Africa Printing and Publishing House (SAPPHO) (Pvt) Ltd, 95 Harare Street, Harare, Zimbabwe

Cover Design by Hassan Musa

Printed by Strand Multiprint, Harare, Zimbabwe

ISBN 1-77905-012-7

Contents

Nation-Building and State Building in Africa

This paper was originally written in 1988 in response to an invitation by the African Academy of Sciences for a keynote address to the Fourth Symposium of the Special Commission on Africa in Harare on "The Idea of Nation-Building: Its Western Origins and African Implications." I am publishing it five years later with minor modifications due to changing circumstances for purposes of stimulating debate on nation-building and state-building in Africa. These are issues of vital importance to our continent and, as such, deserve to be analyzed scientifically for purposes of understanding them better and providing policy makers the ways and means of dealing with them appropriately.

I must say, at the outset, that I reject the notion that the idea of nation-building is somehow a "Western" idea. Does its "Western origin" refer to the emergence of the modern nation-state based on the capitalist mode of production around 1700 in Europe, with a bourgeois-type of state characterized by formal equality before the law and a secular legal-rational order?[1] Or does it refer to the very idea of the existence of a relatively large political community beyond the family and tribal settlements in which there obtains an orderly exercise of authority based on a shared understanding between rulers and ruled on their reciprocal rights and obligations?[2] Obviously, the title cannot refer to the latter case, but it is still prone to creating confusion about political ideas in general and the idea of nation-building in particular.

We should be careful not to give Europeans or Westerners the monopoly on political ideas. The English historian C. Northcote Parkinson, who is best known as the author of the Parkinson's Law of bureaucratic organization, has warned us not to believe that "all political thinking has been done in Europe and America,"[3] or to attribute the origin of democracy and other political ideas to the Greeks. In his book *The Evolution of Political Thought*, he introduces the chapter on "the origins of democracy" as follows:

> In commenting upon the course of history, St. Augustine is shrewd enough to suggest (as did Sallust before him) that the Athenians exceeded other people more in their publicity than in their deeds. Most subsequent scholars have been more credulous, one result being a surprisingly widespread belief that the Athenians were the inventors of democracy. That they were nothing of the kind is tolerably clear. What we owe to the Athenians is not the thing itself or even its name but the earliest detailed account of how a

democracy came into being, flourished and collapsed. Of the Indian democracies, which were probably older, we have all too little precise information. There is, however, a sense in which many people have had a measure of democracy in their village life.[4]

Among the people who knew democracy at the village level and, indeed, beyond the village, were our ancestors in pre-colonial Africa. These people did have political ideas, including those of expanding the political space beyond kinship groups and enhancing the capacity of the state to govern the larger territory in an effective way. I would contend that Shaka the Zulu, the builders of Great Zimbabwe, the Ndebele king Lobengula, the Mbundu princess Nzinga, Kalala Ilunga of the Luba, King Ghezo of Dahomey and many other rulers of pre-colonial Africa were nation-builders. And they built, or attempted to build, nations without the benefit of Western ideas.

Likewise, the African people learned the lessons of resistance to colonial rule from their own history, not from the history of the West. In a now famous essay on "The Relevance of 'Western Ideas' for the New African States,"[5] Thomas Hodgkin rejects the thesis advanced by Rupert Emerson that "it was from European history that the lessons of the struggle for freedom could on the whole be most effectively learned" by Asian and African nationalists.[6] According to Hodgkin, this is wrong not only in its minimization of the role of the popular masses in the African independence struggle, but also because of its ethnocentrism:

> For large masses of Africans in a variety of colonial territories to say "no" to the colonial system and "yes" to the ideas of "freedom" and "independence" it was not an essential pre-requisite that their leaders should have studied the Western political classics at Harvard, the Sorbonne, or the London School of Economics.[7]

The Western Origin of Contemporary Social Science and Policy Analysis

Having said that, I do recognize that modern social science is an academic discipline of Western creation for which European history and the history of Western philosophy constitute its strongest foundations. Many of the terms commonly used by social scientists around the world are deeply rooted in the Western intellectual tradition. This is true of both of the major tendencies in social science today: the more conventional paradigm based on Weberian sociology and Marxism or historical materialism. In spite of the latter's rightful claim to universality as a revolutionary science of society and history, V. I. Lenin defined Marxism with respect to its Western intellectual roots and content as combining the best of German philosophy, English political economy and French socialism.[8]

It is therefore necessary to separate the Eurocentricity of both mainstream social science and Marxism from their wider applicability as scientific tools of analysis. This latter, and more universal, aspect of the Western intellectual tradition is definitely relevant to the analysis of the political economy of the state and nation-building in Africa. To apply the tools of political economy and policy analysis in a way that would clarify the salient issues of national construction, governance and public policy, we need a comparative perspective and some knowledge of how these issues were addressed by social theorists in the past.

In an essay on the intellectual history of policy analysis, David Garson argues that the search for a more relevant theoretical basis for this discipline — and one that would satisfy both empirical and normative concerns — must start with a survey of the past.[9] "Ironically," he writes, "the way forward for policy analysis may lie in a closer examination of its past as represented by social theorists like Lasswell, Merriam, and even earlier, Weber and Marx."[10] Without denying the fundamental contribution of the last two theorists to contemporary social science and policy analysis, I would contend that one needs to go further back in order to gain a better knowledge of the Western origin of these disciplines and a more comprehensive picture of the universal issues of nation-building and state capacity building.

The list of political theorists before Marx and Weber should include Plato and Aristotle, among the theorists of the Greek city-state; the great African theologian St. Augustine and St. Thomas Aquinas, among the theorists of the universal Christian community; and Niccolo Machiavelli, Jean Bodin, Thomas Hobbes, John Locke, Montesquieu and Jean-Jacques Rousseau, among the theorists of the European nation-state.[11] Rather than doing a full survey of the contribution of each of these authors, I will limit myself to brief comments on the major epistemological breaks and thematic developments that have helped to shape the methodological and conceptual framework of contemporary social science and policy analysis.

It is widely accepted today that a new science of politics, empirical and comparative in nature, began with Aristotle. A former student of Plato, he rejected the utopian enterprise of his teacher for an empirical and descriptive search for the general historical conditions likely to ensure the good functioning of a state. The epistemological break between the two has been described as follows:

Plato believed that in politics it was possible to establish principles having the precision and certainty of mathematics, whereas Aristotle believed that in politics, as in biology, careful and patient empirical inquiry was the only way of arriving at reliable generalizations. Plato believed that the apprehension of the Form of the Good would reveal exactly how a community ought to be organized and governed, whereas Aristotle thought that the right organization for any given state could only be discovered by careful examination of its other characteristics.[12]

The preservation of a satisfactory political order, rather than moral perfection, was Aristotle's basic principle of politics, according to which the state has to be capable of satisfying the material and spiritual needs of its citizens. At the same time, Aristotle's science-based theory of politics was not devoid of normative considerations. Like Plato, he was also interested in the practical aspects of the science of politics, and he served as a tutor to the Macedonian prince Alexander, who later became the warrior and empire-builder known as Alexander the Great.

Preoccupied with the question of how to prevent instability and revolution, Aristotle could not avoid producing his own theory of the best political regime. For him, the best regime is that in which the middle class holds political power. Much of Anglo-Saxon political theory has been influenced by this and other Aristotelian ideas. Seymour Martin Lipset's views on the "pre-conditions for democracy" are a good example of Aristotle's influence today.[13]

The second major epistemological break in the evolution of Western political thought was due to the work of Machiavelli. With him, the break was significant at two levels: the secularization of political theory, by its divorce from metaphysics and religion, and the exaltation of the modern nation-state as a sovereign political entity above the individual, the self-governing city-state and even the universal community of medieval conceptions. The historical significance of his break with religion can be seen in the fact that "Machiavelli's indifference to the truth of religion became in the end a common characteristic of modern thought, but it was emphatically not true of the two centuries after he wrote."[14]

If Aristotle had conceived the city-state as a natural and supreme form of political association higher than the family and the tribe, Machiavelli gave primacy to the modern nation-state as an organization of force for the control of a given territory and its defence against both external aggression and internal subversion. He is, by virtue of this conception, his hostility against the feudal aristocracy and his support for the rising bourgeoisie and a strong central government under an absolute monarch, the theoretician par *excellence* of nation-building and the modern nation-state. For him, political science is a scientifically-based statecraft designed to identify the most effective *means* with which to attain political *ends*. The primary end of politics — and according to Machiavelli, one based on the fundamental human demand for security — is "the creation and maintenance of a strong, united and expanding state."[15]

Machiavelli's advice on what it takes to acquire power and to defend it against all encroachments has had a lot of success with rulers and policy makers worldwide, far beyond the Italian nation-state of his dreams. With him, there emerged a tradition of treating the study of politics as a purely technical matter, and policy analysis as simply a handmaiden of government. For many African rulers and their external backers, the stability that the colonialists were able to maintain is likely to disappear after independence, under the weight of centrifugal forces, unless these destabilizing forces are checked by strongarm rule. In general, the Western prescription for order in Africa during much of the post-colonial period was rule by Machiavellian strongmen who would stop at nothing to attain their objectives and serve Western interests.[16]

The two centuries separating Machiavelli's work from that of Montesquieu were marked by the development of the theory of the nation-state and its companion, the theory of sovereignty. The latter theory consisted of two levels: (1) the *sovereignty of the state* or the idea of its independent existence internationally and its dominance over all other groupings and organizations, within its territory, and (2) the *sovereignty of state power* or the specific rights and privileges of rulers in relation to the ruled. With the nation-state firmly established as a historical fact in Europe, it was the second level of sovereignty that retained the attention of political theorists.

The critical question was no longer that of founding the nation-state, but of balancing the conflicting social forces within an already established and strong state.[17] At the same time, for theorists like Bodin in France and Hobbes in England, it was still necessary to consider the question of the consent of the ruled to absolute monarchy, the sovereignty of the latter being posed as a categorical imperative of the existence and survival of a stable political order.

With Montesquieu, as with Locke before him, concern with absolute power gives way to greater interest in the balancing of social forces and to the ideal of limited power. According to Maurice Durerger, Montesquieu's

L'Esprit des lois (1978) is "the first treatise of political sociology."[18] Building on the foundation of political science laid by Aristotle, Machiavelli and Bodin, Montesquieu proceeds from the facts — the laws and customs of various people — and not values in an attempt to elaborate a historical classification of the forms of state. He seeks to establish a linkage between political institutions and peoples on the one hand, and their milieu on the other, with particular emphasis on the climate.

Montesquieu's theory of political regimes, according to which the dominant social ideal determines the principal form of rule, is not as widely known as his theory of the separation of powers, or the joint attribution of sovereign power to three organs of government. Contrary to popular belief, Montesquieu did not propose it as a judicial theory of government. His is a sociological theory designed to preserve social equilibrium through the joint sovereignty of three social forces: the king, ordinary people, and the aristocracy. The American Federalists (John Adams, Alexander Hamilton, and James Madison) were to seize upon this idea of the distribution of political power in society, but proceeded to vest sovereign power in three branches of government — the executive, legislature and judiciary — related to one another through checks and balances.

The last great theorist of the social contract and the last major figure in the development of an empirically-based science of politics before Karl Marx was Jean-Jacques Rousseau. More radical in his analysis of the state and civil society than Locke and Montesquieu, Rousseau used the comparative method to show the influence of society over the individual, the relationship between civil society and property ownership, and the linkage between political authority and the maintenance of inequality. He saw property ownership as a source of evil and inequality and the state as a creation of the rich designed to maintain their position as a dominant class and to preserve inequality.[19]

Many of the ideas of his *Discourse on Political Economy* (1755) have pre-Marxist themes that were later underlined by Frederick Engels, whose book *The Origin of the Family, Private Property and the State* (1884) drew inspiration from Rousseau's analysis of social development.

On the perennial question of forms of rule, Rousseau refused to choose the best regime. But, in a passage of his best known book, *On the Social Contract* (1762), that has been characterized as one of "the first faint glimmerings of scientific thought" in the long history of political philosophy,[20] he offers an empirical test for determining a good or bad government:

What is the object of political association? It is the preservation and prosperity of its members. And what is the surest sign that they are preserved and prosperous? It is their number and population. Do not, then, go and seek elsewhere for this sign so much discussed. All other things being equal, the government under which, without external aids, without naturalization and without colonies, the citizens increase and multiply most, is infallibly the best. That under which a people diminishes and decays is the worst. Statisticians, it is now your business; reckon, measure, compare.[21]

In this age of birth control, such a test will have to focus more on the quality of life than on the size of the population. For the best measure of decay today is not so much the reduction in numbers as the evils of malnutrition, disease, unsanitary living conditions, lack of economic opportunity, and the state's violation of the political, economic, social and cultural rights of citizens.

This is where the contribution of Karl Marx is most relevant to social analysis. For him, the role of radical social theory is to assess the possibilities of changing social reality from the perspective of ordinary people and to promote radical change in their favour. Public policy reflects the social relations of production and it is by changing these relations in a manner consistent with the needs of the popular masses that the state can be made to serve their interests.

Marx, like Rousseau, begins his analysis with the class structure of civil society. It is with reference to the fundamental reality that class relations constitute in modern society and to the class struggle as a dynamic factor of historical change that Marx and Engels founded historical materialism. This is a science that seeks to apprehend historical reality not from the standpoint of the dominant classes, who have a vested interest in mystifying the way society works, but from the perspective of ordinary people, who have nothing to lose from truthful analyses of their predicament. Barrington Moore has suggested that this latter perspective comes closer to objective scientific analysis:

For all students of human society, sympathy with the victims of historical processes and skepticism about the victors' claims provide essential safeguards against being taken in by the dominant mythology. A scholar who tries to be objective needs these feelings as part of his ordinary working equipment.[22]

Over the past 100 years, all substantial contributions to political theory have been made in an attempt to disprove or develop Marxism as a science. V. I. Lenin, Rosa Luxemburg, Antonio Gramsci and Mao Zedong are the leading figures among those who saw Marxism not as a dogma but a living theory that never ceases to develop itself further. They each attempted to sharpen its analytical tools and to apply its scientific method to new realities. A limited but outstanding contribution in this respect was also made by Amilcar Cabral in his application of the theory of the national liberation struggle to an African context.

On the opposite side, students of social theory will agree with Alvin Gouldner that much of the history of contemporary Western social science is "unintelligible except as a response to and a polemic against Marxism."[23] The work of Vilfredo Pareto, Gaetano Mosca, Max Weber, Robert Michels, Arthur Bently and the American-dominated modernization school is characterized by direct or indirect confrontation with Marxism. Although there are important differences in approach and emphasis, with modernization being variously defined in economic, sociological, psychological or political terms, most of the modernization theorists share an intellectual debt to Max Weber's theory of the state and his use of conceptual polarities and topological methods, an ethnocentric vision of development in non-Western societies as becoming more like the West, and an emphasis on the positive role of the neo-colonial elites as agents of social change.[24]

My own preference is for the Marxist tendency of the Western intellectual tradition, as enriched by Third World contributions that enhance its universality as a scientific tool of analysis. Marxism in its orthodox and Eurocentric conceptions shares with modernization theory an inability to apprehend social reality and to explain the process of nation-building in Africa in an adequate manner. In the remainder of this paper, I will attempt to formulate an appropriate way of looking at the political economy of the state and nation-building in Africa. As I have already suggested in my book *Revolution and Counter-Revolution in Africa*,[25] — from which I will draw freely — the critical issues of national construction, governance and public policy in Africa today are not intelligible outside of the general context of the continuing struggle for national liberation. For they are part and parcel of the relationship between the national liberation struggle and the class struggle, of the dialectic between revolution and counter-revolution, in post-colonial Africa. I shall begin with a discussion of the concept of a nation.

What is a Nation?

"The central fact of nation-building," Reinhard Bendix writes, "is the orderly exercise of a nationwide, public authori'y."[26] There is no debate today as to whether or not an orderly exercise of authority did obtain in the political communities of the pre-modern era, including those of pre-colonial Africa. The pertinent question is to determine at what point in time did these communities become nations, and how the states governing them managed to extend their authority nationwide, over the entire territory. Both modernization theory and orthodox Marxism identify this point with the emergence of the modern nation-state in Europe. From this point of view, nationhood and nation-building are basically novel ideas for much of the African continent.

Influenced by this view, the Western news media continue to portray Africa as a continent whose arbitrarily-created countries are rent by ancient tribal enmities that complicate and retard the development of national consciousness. Moreover, they tend to explain all African political crises in terms of "tribalism" defined as attachment to one's tribe or ethnic group, which remains a more relevant unit of identification than the country as a whole.

This image of Africa was given scientific respectability in the early 1960s by Clifford Geertz's thesis that "primordial" sentiments were the most relevant factor of social reality in the newly independent countries.[27] This thesis was enthusiastically applied to Africa by modernization theorists like David Apter and Aristide Zolberg.[28] Apter saw the "tribal system" as being in conflict with modern (i.e., Western) patterns of social and political organization.[29] A former student of Apter's, Zolberg saw the state as lacking the capacity to exercise its authority over the ethnically-determined space of civil society at the local level.[30] In a position similar to Samuel Huntington's view of political decay,[31] he came to the conclusion that the new African states were suffering from too little rather than too much authority.[32] Unlike Huntington, who recommended a Leninist-type of party organization as the best tool for nation-building and order, Zolberg advocated the creation of American-style political machines as means of maintaining stability.

Two decades later, the thesis of "primordial sentiments" has been revived by Goran Hyden, who refers to primordial ties of solidarity as "the economy of affection."[33] This is defined as a peculiar type of peasant economy comprising multiple and discrete networks of "support, communications, and interactions among structurally defined groups connected by blood, kin, community or other affinities, for example religion."[34]

According to Hyden, Africa will in due time evolve from tribal to non-tribal society, from mechanic to organic solidarity, from ascriptive-oriented behaviour to an achievement-oriented one, and from the economy of affection to a legal-rational economic order. There are no shortcuts to development. The only development strategy necessary for effecting a successful transition, and the one Hyden proposes, is to strengthen an indigenous capitalist bourgeoisie unfettered by state regulations and left free to wage a deadly battle against pre-capitalist structures and mentalities. Peasant power, interests and autonomy must be sacrificed for the sake of national development. The modern nation is born through the passing away of traditional society.[35]

By granting an *a priori* determinism to blood, kinship, religion and other "primordial" ties, loyalties and affinities, Hyden joins other modernization theorists in obscuring the interplay of class, economic and geo-political factors which weigh heavily on contemporary African politics. His analysis is also guilty of a serious methodological flaw. He insists, on the one hand, that Africa is a unique or special case to be analyzed differently from other parts of the world. And yet, on the other hand, he maintains an evolutionary perspective, according to which Africa will some day look like the West. The flaw resides in the fact that, contrary to the purported uniqueness of Africa and the need to analyze it with original theories and concepts, it is the same old modernization theory with its dichotomous vision of tradition and modernity that is being applied to Africa.[36]

It should not come as a surprise that Orthodox Marxism, being itself a product of the Western intellectual tradition, should pose the question of nationhood in terms so similar to those of bourgeois social science. Like modernization theorists, orthodox Marxists assume that the nation is a social phenomenon produced by the development of capitalism. Their understanding of the national question is primarily, if not exclusively, based on their reading of Joseph Stalin's *Marxism and the National Question* (1913), in which he defines the nation as "*a historically constituted, stable community of people, formed on the basis of a common language, territory, economic life, and psychological make-up manifested in a common culture.*"[37] For Stalin, such a community requires for its viability an integrated home market and, consequently, belongs to the epoch of rising capitalism.

The four characteristic features delineated by Stalin are not to be used mechanically as a checklist against which nationhood is to be gauged.[38] They have to be seen as necessary rather than sufficient conditions of nationhood, for they can also be found in social formations based on pre-capitalist modes of production. What is sufficient to make a nation, Stalin's followers argue, is the "particular historical practice that produces those features as a unity — the formation of distinct capitalist social formations."[39] Why, it may be asked, is capitalism the only mode of production capable of grafting these features on a socio-historical entity to produce a nation? Is it impossible to achieve the centralization of economic organization and political authority essential to nationhood under other modes of production? Stalin's followers have no satisfactory answers to these questions other than appealing to European history, which is their point of reference.

Nicos Poulantzas and Samir Amin have made extremely pertinent critiques of this orthodox theory of the nation.[40] Poulantzas castigates the profoundly empiricist and positivist conception of the constituent elements of a nation in this theory and raises doubts about the usefulness of the central argument that the nation is a creation of merchant capital:

> The generalization of commercial exchange cannot explain the creation of the modern nation; if it reveals the necessity of the unification of the so-called internal market and the elimination of obstacles to the circulation of goods and capital, it does not in any way explain why this unification takes place precisely at the level of the nation.[41]

Samir Amin's views on the national question evolved from less rigid formulations in the early to mid-1970s to more orthodox positions in the late 1970s. Contrary to his earlier formulations in *Unequal Development,* where he allows for "at least an embryonic stage of national development" for the tributary and trading formations of black Africa,[42] and in *The Arab Nation*, where he defines the phenomenon of nationhood in a more universalistic perspective, he seems to have moved closer to the orthodox Marxist theory in a later book, *Class and Nation*.[43] Here, he limits the appearance of nations to two types of society: "complete tributary" and "capitalist societies."[44] Most of the tributary formations of black Africa are thereby excluded, as they were "incomplete" and lacking in "irreversible state formation," which seems to be tied to the use of animal energy in agriculture and of writing.[45] Needless to say, it is his earlier formulations which retain our attention here.

In *The Arab Nation*, Amin attacks the orthodox theory for confusing the existence of nations with one of its historical expressions, namely, the emergence of nation-states in Europe in connection with the development of capitalism.[46] This does not allow for a full understanding of the phenomenon of nationhood in other parts of the world because orthodox theory assumes that nations cannot exist in the absence of capitalist development:

> According to these assumptions, nations would only exist at the centre of the world capitalist system, in the areas where the bourgeois revolution has established the national power of the local bourgeoisie. Elsewhere nations would not actually exist, at least not in the finished form. What then are we to say of the social realities of the pre-capitalist world, where an old statist tradition blends into a cultural and linguistic reality? Thousand-year old Egypt has always been united on the level of language, culture and — except during some brief periods of decadence — on the level of political power as well. Whilst it is not a bourgeois nation, it is certainly something more than an incongruous and unorganized conglomerate of peoples. Furthermore, even those regions which were not organized into unified and centralized states, and which were not united culturally and linguistically, have increasingly become so following upon their integration into the international capitalist system as colonies or as dominated semi-dependent countries. Even if this unification has not been the work of a national bourgeoisie it is nonetheless an important social fact.[47]

It follows then, that as a social phenomenon the nation is not necessarily or exclusively a product of the capitalist mode of production. It may appear at other stages of history as a particular unit of reproduction which requires a centralization of economic organization and political authority, and such centralization is best achieved through state power. This is why there is a dialectical relationship between state and nation in the modern world. The nation either emerges to coincide with an existing state, or consolidates itself as a modern nation by creating its own state.[48]

The relationship between the two is mediated through two matrices which constitute the material framework of institutions and social practices: the spatial matrix of territory and geographic contiguity, and the temporal matrix of a shared historical and cultural tradition.[49] Both matrices are necessary conditions of the existence of a nation as well as factors that the state and/or the social class playing the unifying role of political and economic centralization can manipulate to promote among the people a greater sense of collective identification with the nation as a socio-historical entity larger and more meaningful than their locality or regional groupings. Such a promotion is the work of all institutions belonging to, or subject to the influence of, the state system, including education, cultural and religious organizations.

The phenomenon of nationhood is both reversible and variable with respect to its intensity. The level of nationhood may be more or less intense depending on the development of the productive forces and the impact of the state's role in the material organization of time and space on the constituent elements of the nation. With more resources and well-equipped armies, bureaucracies, prisons, schools and other institutions with which to fashion the nation, advanced capitalism does have better conditions for sustaining a stronger or more intense level of nationhood than pre-capitalist and underdeveloped societies.

Samir Amin's proposition that "the phenomenon of nationhood is a reversible process," whereby a nation may develop and grow stronger or "regress into a formless conglomeration of more or less related ethnic groups,"[50] is particularly applicable to these societies.

The Formation of Nations in Africa

These reflections do allow us to place the national question as it relates to Africa in its proper perspective. In pre-colonial Africa, there were nations at different levels of intensity corresponding to social formations made up of closely related lineages or other kinship groups unified by a core cultural tradition and a relatively durable politico-administrative structure. These formations were held together by ruling classes based on tribute collection and which succeeded in promoting the growth of long-distance trade, protecting markets and trade routes, and ensuring the centralization and redistribution of the surplus. The myths of origin, ideologies of kingship and the oral histories of migrations and conquests were instrumental in creating for these ruling classes a cultural tradition that served to cement a national identity and to help galvanize political loyalty and support among their peoples. The national fact was so real for some of these societies, that even after their disintegration as a result of external conquest and colonial rule, serious attempts were to be made to revive them in the post-colonial period.

It must be emphasized, however, that not all pre-colonial states corresponded to or overlapped with nations. In Central Africa, for example, there were trade and conquest states that did not exhibit nationality characteristics as developed over two or more centuries in those entities like Kongo, Kuba, Luba and Lunda kingdoms which emerged as relatively viable nations.[51]

Unlike these nations, the trade and conquest states were heterogenous entities lacking a distinctive cultural tradition linking the state to a people with deep historical roots in the territory. These states included Queen Nzinga's Kingdom of Matamba, the Imbangala Kingdom of Kasanje, the expansionist Lunda Kingdom of Kazembe, and the Nyamwezi/Yeke Kingdom of Garenganze.[52]

With the colonial conquest and occupation, the potential of African social formations to develop viable nations was greatly diminished. Those nations which existed at the time of the conquest lost their vitality, if not their very existence, as nations. The intensity of nationhood depended on the structure of the colonial state: stronger where the latter corresponded to a historical state — as in Burundi, Egypt, Lesotho, Libya, Madagascar, Morocco, Rwanda, Swaziland, Tunisia, and Zanzibar — and weaker where it incorporated different nationalities and groups.

In the latter case, the traditional rulers were to serve as subordinate agents of local colonial administration as well as representatives of their subjects *vis-à-vis* the colonial state. Whether the method of colonial rule was said to be direct or indirect, they performed their administrative tasks in a more satisfactory manner than they were ever able to defend the interests of their people.[53] These tasks were chiefly extractive and regulatory in nature: revenue collection, labor recruitment, conscription, forced labour on public projects, compulsory cultivation of certain export crops, law and order, and the enforcement of public health and other state regulations. Alienated from their traditional rulers, ordinary people had to seek a new leadership in their struggle against colonialism. They found it in the new African *petit-bourgeoisie*, the class that was to become the standard-bearer of modern African nationalism.

The impact of colonialism on the national question was thus a complex one. On the one hand, the imposition of colonial rule resulted in the fading away of a large number of pre-colonial nations, or their disintegration into that "formless conglomeration of more or less related ethnic groups" described by Samir Amin. On the other hand, colonialism united different African nationalities and peoples under a single territorial and institutional framework, widened their social space as a result of greater inter-ethnic interaction through the institutions and practices of the colonial system, and thus created a common historical experience of economic exploitation, political and administrative oppression, and cultural oppression.[54]

Africans experienced capitalist exploitation and colonial oppression as blacks or as Arabs, and this experience had a lot to do with their response to the colonial situation. Denied their human and democratic rights, they were also victims of discriminatory practices with regard to economic and social justice: lack of equal employment opportunities, investment credit, property rights, access to the better social services and amenities reserved for Europeans, etc. Consequently, it was their common identification of the colonial society as the general obstacle to social and economic progress that made it possible for all social classes to unite in a common struggle against colonialism.

In black Africa, this struggle was also inspired by the fight against racism and oppression in the African diaspora of North America and the Caribbean, home of the intellectual pioneers of pan-Africanism (H. Sylvester Williams, W.E.B. DuBois, Marcus Garvey). As an intellectual movement, pan-Africanism represented the rise to self-assertion of Africans and peoples of African descent outside the continent with the overriding goal to regain their social dignity as a people and to establish eventually an independent nation in the African homeland. This was especially true for Garveyism, the prophetic and mass-based wing of the movement, whose influence was felt all over black Africa.[55]

With pan-Africanism, the national question became more complex, as political entrepreneurs or would-be founders of nations had to grapple with the problem of determining the most relevant socio-historical entity to develop as a nation. Which one of the following three entities was the new African nation to correspond to: (1) the *ethnic nation* of ancient glory whose construction was arrested by colonialism, or the one born out of the contradictions of the colonial situation (e.g., Luba Kasai, Igbo); (2) the colonially-created *territorial nation*; or (3) the *pan-African nation*, of which diaspora Africans were to be a part? Each of the three positions had its defenders, including the first which received a passionate though unconvincing defence in Chief Obafemi Awolowo's 1947 book, *Path to Nigerian Freedom*, in which he argues for a multi-national state based on a federation of ethnic nations.[56] At the other end of the spectrum were politicians like Kwame Nkrumah, who advocated a pan-African entity and proposed the creation of a "United States of Africa."[57]

Generally it can be said that the pan-African ideal, however attractive it might have been to African nationalists between 1945 and 1960, was in flagrant contradiction with both the neo-colonialist strategy of imperialism and the class interests of the African *petit-bourgeoisie*, the class leading the nationalist struggle. The basic thrust of neo-colonialism was for the imperialist powers to grant independence to the colonial territories while retaining control over their economies in order to keep these countries within the world capitalist system as indispensable sources of raw materials and cheap labour for the imperialist countries. Amilcar Cabral has described the imperialist strategy of decolonization as follows:

> The objective of the imperialist countries is to prevent the enlargement of the socialist camp, to liberate the reactionary forces in our countries which were being stifled by colonialism and to enable these forces to ally themselves with the international bourgeoisie. The fundamental objective was to create a bourgeoisie where one did not exist, in order specifically to strengthen the imperialist and the capitalist camp.[58]

The aims and objectives of imperialism were basically compatible with the class interests of the African *petit-bourgeoisie*. Both the imperialists and the African nationalist leaders opted for the dismantling of the colonial empires into their constituent territories, as these would prove easier to manipulate and to control from the standpoint of the imperialists, and provide a more fertile terrain for the advancement of the economic and political interests of the *petit-bourgeoisie*. Balkanization gave even mediocre leaders the chance to become heads of state or cabinet ministers at the national level, something that might have escaped them altogether within larger and more complex units.

Consistent with this process of balkanization, administratively centralized units that were under the control of a single governor-general, like French West Africa, French Equatorial Africa, and the Belgian Congo and Ruanda-Urundi were split up into eight, four and three countries respectively.

Efforts to retain French West Africa as a single entity or to salvage the larger portion of it into a federation were sabotaged by the French imperialists, with the help of African politicians like Félix Houphouet-Boigny, a major leader of the region-wide nationalist movement, the *Rassemblement Démocratique Africain* (RDA). Radical parties in Guinea, French Sudan (Mali), and Niger joined progressive elements in Senegal, Upper Volta (Burkina Faso) and Dahomey (Benin) to keep up the fight for unity, but lost. The pan-African ideal had fallen victim to imperialism and *petit-bourgeois* opportunism. As Walter Rodney writes, the African *petit-bourgeoisie* reneged on a cardinal principle of pan-Africanism: namely, the unity and indivisibility of the African continent.[59]

Thus did the concept of the nation become attached to the territorial entities of the colonial partition, not as a matter of necessity in the organization of the anti-colonial struggle, as Crawford Young maintains,[60] but as a result of the interplay of imperialist and African *petit-bourgeois* interests. The year 1956 can be taken as a benchmark in the annals of

African territorial nationalism. It was not only the year of the Suez crisis and the preservation of Egypt's independence and national sovereignty, but also the year of: (1) the independence of Morocco, Tunisia and Sudan; (2) the *loi-cadre* establishing territorial governments in the French colonies of West Africa, Equatorial Africa and Madagascar; and (3) the emergence of modern nationalist politics in Zaire, Angola and Guinea-Bissau.[61]

By 1958, when the All-African Peoples Conference was held in Accra, Ghana, the talk of a pan-African nation had become a rhetorical exercise. Most delegates were representatives of nationalist movements seeking the independence of their respective colonial territories. Territorial nationalism had established itself so strongly as a norm that one of the delegates was pressured to abandon the "tribal anachronism" of his movement. The delegate in question was Holden Roberto, then representative of the Union of the People of Northern Angola (UPNA), which he renamed overnight in response to this pressure as the Union of the People of Angola (UPA). The UPNA was the political voice of the separatist movement of the Kongo of Angola, which had sought to restore the old Kongo Kingdom.[62]

The pressure on Roberto in Accra was symptomatic of the new African commitment to build new nations out of the arbitrarily created colonial territories.

On the whole, the political map of Africa represents a double failure: the failure of the pan-African ideal of a single nation under one continental state or under several regional federations; and that of reactionary nationalism, which had sought to recreate or revive pre-colonial nations. Both the pan-African nation and the pre-colonial nation did not have well-organized class forces capable of realizing them as political projects. It was shown above that the *petit-bourgeois* intellectuals who once championed pan-Africanism quickly embraced the European architects of decolonization to become "fathers" of their respective territorial nations. As for the "natural" rulers of Africa, their alienation from the mass of the people in most colonial territories was irreversible.

The new African nation was born in the struggle against colonialism. It had its class base in the African *petit-bourgeoisie*, the class to whose interests it corresponded within the colonized society. In addition to the *petit-bourgeoisie*, the proletarianized and semi-proletarianized masses had also before independence developed some emotional identification with this new socio-historical entity.[63] This is especially true of those fractions of these classes which had become urbanized and which had migrated to urban and industrial centres out of their areas of origin. Their class interests as workers and informal sector entrepreneurs were better served within a territorial entity in which they both felt at home and in which they did not have to compete with too many other people for jobs, resources and means of livelihood. Thus, if the *petit-bourgeoisie* was the standard-bearer of territorial nationalism, these class fractions were among its most active supporters.

Most countries of the African continent are arbitrary colonial creations. Of the 54 internationally recognized entities (the 52 OAU members plus Morocco and South Africa), only 10 correspond to historical states while four others have a clearly defined cultural identity. The first group, already identified above, includes Ethiopia, but not Zanzibar, which is now part of the United Republic of Tanzania. The second group consists of Algeria, Botswana, Somalia and Western Sahara.[64]

With few exceptions, the other 40 states each comprise a mixture of peoples without a core cultural tradition around which all others may coalesce. For these countries, national construction involves the development of a multi-ethnic entity based on a common history of colonial oppression and a common commitment to forging a new cultural identity linked to all the traditions of the past without at the same time being strongly attached to one of them.[65] Most of the historical states and other pre-colonial political entities are also faced with this challenge, inasmuch as the state itself is linked to a dominant cultural tradition that has been imposed on peripheral groups and minorities: the Ethiopian state *vis-à-vis* non-Amhara groups like the Oromo, Arab-controlled Algeria *vis-à-vis* the Berbers, etc.

The process of national construction must therefore reflect the commitment to unity in diversity. This implies not only the need to integrate all the common traits of all cultures in order to forge a new historical identity, but also a scrupulous respect for the language, originality and specificity of each group. Such respect is essential to national unity, particularly in those countries where one or several major groups may assert their cultural and political dominance at the expense of minorities. It is essential also to the task of mobilizing progressive forces to continue the struggle against imperialist domination through neo-colonialism. By destroying this domination, the country resolves the national question by achieving a greater ability to freely determine its own destiny and to transform the economy so it may serve the interests of workers and peasants.

Governance and Public Policy

An essential aspect of nation-building is state-capacity building — i.e., enhancing the capacity of the state not only to establish its authority throughout the national territory but also to serve the economic, social and cultural needs of citizens. According to Parkinson, if there is one important idea to emerge from the history of political thought, it is "the idea that government is to be judged by results."[66] And a good government, as Rousseau suggested, is that which improves the quality of life of its people. Its legitimacy and the people's sense of identification with the political order are likely to be enhanced by good performance in this regard. The present crisis of the state in Africa, or its declining capacity for stability and development, is related to its failure to satisfy the needs and aspirations of ordinary people.

The basic issue with respect to governance and public policy in Africa today is the extent to which governments are able to satisfy their people's expectations of independence, namely, their sincere hope that freedom from colonial rule would usher in a new era of basic rights and freedoms long denied under foreign or settler rule. This is what the liberation struggle meant for ordinary Africans, as Amilcar Cabral found out while leading the fight for the independence of Guinea-Bissau and Cape Verde. He reminds us in his writings on this experience that ordinary people have a right to expect a better life after all the sacrifices they endured during the liberation struggle. People do not fight for ideas, he writes, but for peace, material benefits, and a better future for their children.[67]

Likewise, Professor J. F. Ade Ajayi, a distinguished African historian, has summed up the meaning of independence for the African masses as follows:

Insofar as they fully appreciated what was involved in the independence movements, their basic expectation was to see an end to the unpredictability and irrationality of the white man's world. Without the dubious advantages of Western education, they rejected the white man's culture, and for as long as possible, stuck to what they knew. This did not mean that they wanted to recreate the past in its entirety. Their notion of freedom was not an abstract ideal, but a catalogue of specific wants: freedom from unjust and incomprehensible laws and directives; return of their land; and freedom to be left alone to live their lives and seek their own goals, especially in regard to land tenure and local government groupings that affected historical relationships. These wants developed and became more specific with each new hope and each disastrous frustration. Soon, expectations came to include improved standards of living in housing and clothing, greater returns for their labor, better transportation for exporting and marketing their surpluses, education as a means to the social mobility that would ensure a better life for their children, and an adequate water supply, electricity, health-care facilities, and other such amenities of life.[68]

These popular aspirations eventually came into sharp conflict with the interests of the *petit-bourgeois* nationalists who led the struggle for independence. Initially, the intellectual elite among them had expressed commitment to the ideals of democracy, economic development, and pan-African unity. For the most part, however, these intellectual aspirations gave way to narrow class interests. They were eventually replaced by new commitments, chief among which were a fascination with politics as an exciting and lucrative career, an emphasis not on abstract ideals but on concrete material gains in power and wealth, and a devotion to territorial nationalism instead of pan-Africanism. As politicians, and later on military officers, vied with each other to acquire power and wealth as well as to do everything possible to retain them, a very limited supply of governmental energy and resources would be made available for development purposes.[69]

The independence struggle had masked the conflicts of interests between the masses and their *petit-bourgeois* leaders. These conflicts became manifest after independence when, instead of fulfilling the people's expectations of freedom and improved living conditions, the new rulers responded to mass grievances with brutal repression. Their agenda was clearly different from the basic aspirations of the masses, being in agreement with popular hopes only at the level of rhetoric. Economic development was and still is a declared priority goal in all countries, but it has seldom been given serious consideration and adequate resources as an operative policy area.

Contrary to a widespread misconception, and one that was entertained by modernization theory, there was no radical change in the state's goal orientation from emphasis on order maintenance under colonialism to an emphasis on development after independence.[70] There is no question that economic development is a major public policy goal to which all modern states subscribe. And it would be foolish for any government, except perhaps one under the control of lunatics, not to be seen as being in favour of improving the quality of life of all citizens. To understand why development has so far remained an elusive goal in Africa, we need to examine its true meaning as well as its deeper significance for the state and civil society in the world today.

Economic development is not to be confused with economic growth, the increase in per capita output of goods and services in a nation's economy. Development refers to a rise in the standard of living of the population in such a way that most people can not only satisfy their economic and social needs more or less adequately, but also enjoy life more fully. This is the true meaning of development as the realization of human personality through the progressive elimination of poverty, unemployment, and inequality.[71] Development thus implies the redistribution of a country's wealth to meet this objective. In its fullest sense, it is not synonymous with economic growth, although growth is its *sine qua non*. It also means much more than satisfying basic needs, even though this is the first step in the right direction.

The deeper significance of this meaning of development for the state and civil society is that development is above all a *political* issue. It involves choice and political will, in addition to contradictions between developed and underdeveloped countries on the one hand, and between social classes within the latter countries on the other. The key question with respect to political will and development choice or strategy involves the interests at stake in the developmental process. Whose interests are to be sacrificed to ensure growth and redistribution? Which social groups are going to bear the major costs of development and which groups stand to reap the major benefits? Answers to these and related questions would help illuminate the state's capacity for development in Africa.

The state in post-colonial Africa is not properly structured to undertake development tasks. As the record on famine relief since 1974 suggest, many a government would gladly entrust the welfare of their people to the so-called international development community, particularly the specialized United Nations agencies and non-governmental organizations (NGOs). But even where a political commitment to development is evident, as in the case of Nyerere's Tanzania, the colonially-inherited structures of the economy and the state act as an obstacle to development, together with the class forces whose interests they promote.[72] Like the colonial state, the post-colonial state is a repressive mechanism in charge of an export-oriented economy that serves primarily those who manage it and their trading and other business partners in the developed countries, at the expense of the welfare of ordinary people. In spite of nationalist and radical ideologies, these people are still being perceived as an ignorant mass with no ideas or wisdom of their own with respect to their economic and social welfare. Consequently, they are seldom consulted on public issues.

With the exception of the rapid expansion of the educational network and the substantial improvement in health services in a number of countries, economic development is clearly subordinated to the other major policy goals of African states, namely, political stability and national security as well as the more extractive and regulative aspects of nation building and state capacity building. A brief analysis of these policy areas should help clarify the major preoccupations and tasks of African governments and thus provide more light on the nature of the state in post-colonial Africa. These areas comprise the bulk of the state's activities in terms of administrative work and revenue allocations. They are discussed in the following two sections on security and defence preoccupations and the state as a structure of control, respectively.

Security and Defence Preoccupations

Political stability and national security constitute a major, if not the most important, preoccupation of the state in post-colonial Africa. According to Crawford Young, the security imperative of contemporary states often takes priority in state revenue allocation and has imposed substantial costs on the post-colonial state in Africa.[73] Not only have the agencies of internal security and external defence claimed the highest or the second highest percentage of government budgets, they have often taken over the running of the state itself. Nearly half of all independent African states are now under either military rule or regimes that initially came to power through military *coup d'état*.[74] Civilian control of the military, a necessary condition of political stability and political change, is still an elusive goal in most African countries.

Popular unrest over unfulfilled expectations and the rising cost of living, the constant threat of military intervention, the crisis of instability associated with the national question, and South Africa's destabilization in Southern Africa have brought security and defence preoccupations to the forefront of the policy agenda. Other contributing factors include the interests of the military as a corporate group and the international environment in which a lucrative arms market and the strategic interests of the major powers have facilitated arms deliveries to Third World countries, with negative consequences for peace and for national construction. For the main effect of the arms race in these countries is to divert resources from economic and social development and to increase their dependence on the major powers, to which they owe billions of dollars for military supplies.[75]

Although the division of the world into two antagonistic social systems represented by the Western and socialist camps, respectively, was a key factor of the arms race and political instability in the Third World, it is the international system itself that has helped to preserve the territorial integrity and national sovereignty of African states. Before the collapse of the Stalinist system in eastern Europe and the former Soviet Union, the world community was committed, in the interests of peace and security, to the survival of the international state system established in the wake of the World War II and the era of decolonization. Apart from the withdrawal of several states from short-lived fusion with their neighbours or from federal arrangements which they found unsatisfactory, the only secession from an existing post-colonial state to win international approval between World War II and 1990 was that which led to the creation of Bangladesh in 1971 out of the eastern portion of Pakistan, itself a result of an earlier balkanization of the former British India.[76] Virtually the whole world went to war through the United Nations organization in 1960-63 to end the Katanga secession and to restore the unity of the Congo (now Zaire).

Support for the principles of territorial integrity and national sovereignty is particularly strong in Africa, where most of the states are militarily weak and must depend on external assistance for their security. States like Chad and Uganda, whose tales of civil war are now legendary, have managed to survive as sovereign entities as a result of both the prevailing climate of opinion in Africa and the world on the necessity of preserving the political map of the continent as drawn by the colonial powers, and the commitment of the warring parties themselves to the survival of the nation-state as constituted at independence. The commitment to this ideal is so strong that what began and lasted for over 20 years as a civil war in Chad was at one point transformed into a war between Chad and Libya, the rival Chadian factions having joined forces to push Libyan troops out of northern Chad.[77] And in Zaire, some of the followers of the former Katangese secessionist leader, Moise Tshombe, re-emerged in 1977-78 to spearhead not another breakaway movement but a national liberation front seeking the overthrow of the Mobutu regime. These are some of the manifestations of the positive appeal of the idea of territorial integrity in Africa.

At the same time, the African continent is so obsessed with its support for internationally recognized boundaries that most of our political and intellectual leaders were so blinded by Ethiopian propaganda that they wrongly condemned the just struggle of the people of Eritrea, whose decolonization was aborted with the complicity of the international community, as a war of secession. The irony of this particular case is that it is absolutely identical to the Western Sahara situation, in which the OAU reaffirmed its cardinal principle of respect for colonially-inherited boundaries.

It must be recognized, however, that the disintegration of the former Soviet Union, Yugoslavia and Czechoslovakia has combined with the worsening of the political climate in Africa to encourage secessionist tendencies or threats from Somalia and Sudan to Zaire and South Africa, with conflicts in the last three cases involving atrocious crimes of genocide in Southern Sudan, ethnic cleansing in the Shaba province of Zaire, and state-sponsored terrorism in South Africa. Ten years after the Sudanese People's Liberation Movement (SPLM) arose as a Southern-based resistance movement seeking a radical transformation of the country as a whole, the Sudan seems to be heading toward a two-state solution. Unlike Somalia, where the former British Somaliland has found no sympathy for its declaration of separate statehood, Africa and the world are likely to support the right of Christian and other non-Muslim Sudanese to resist forced incorporation into Dr. Hassan al-Turabi's militant Islamic state. Ironically, such a development can be shown to be consistent with the colonial legacy, since the roots of the Sudanese crisis are to be found in British colonial policies.[78]

In addition to its significance for the African state system, the colonial legacy has a bearing on national sovereignty. That is to say that it is a salient factor of the extent to which a country is truly independent. Economically, the structure of production and the direction of trade in most countries remain very much the same as under colonialism. African economies are still tied to the economies of the former colonial powers, which continue to exploit the continent's resources through bilateral relations, as in the case of countries of the Franc Zone, or through the multilateral channel of the European Community (EC).[79]

The degree of dependence on the former colonial powers varies in the relation to the economic power and interests of the European countries involved. It is weakest in the former Portuguese and Spanish colonies and strongest in the former French colonies, with the former Belgian and British territories coming somewhere in between. Portugal and Spain were themselves economically underdeveloped colonial powers, and Portugal is still today one of the poorest countries in Western Europe. Spain has greatly evolved to earn the level of "developed country" in current international jargon, but its GNP per capita is much lower than those of most other Western industrialized countries, being within the limits defined by the World Bank for "middle-income developing countries."

The economic backwardness of Portugal was a major reason for its colonial wars in Angola, Mozambique and Guinea-Bissau. Unlike the more developed colonial powers, Portugal had little to gain from decolonization with its major sources of colonial revenues being taxes and royalties from foreign corporations operating in Angola and Mozambique, rather than profits. The neo-colonial option of continued economic domination in a politically independent country was not available to Portugal. Hence its "ultra-colonialism" and the willingness to fight for purposes of retaining the colonies.[80]

In contrast to the prevailing situation in the former British, French, and Belgian territories, the major foreign economic presence in Angola today is not Portuguese. The state draws the bulk of its revenue from the oil extracted by Chevron, a US transnational. At the other extreme are the former French colonies, which have on the whole remained within the grip of French neo-colonialism.[81] Algeria is the major exception in this category. This position is due to a number of factors, including the resource endowment of the country, which is rich in oil, natural gas and other resources, the legacy of the war of national liberation, which produced a highly qualified and confident leadership group, and the positive record of its active support for national liberation movements in Africa and the Arab world.

With few exceptions, the former French colonies of West Africa, Equatorial Africa and the Indian Ocean region from Djibouti to Madagascar are among the most neo-colonial of African post-colonial states. France remains a colonial power in Reunion and in Mayotte, one of the four islands of the independent republic of the Comoros. In spite of its arrogant defiance of OAU resolutions on the total decolonization and the territorial integrity of the Comoro Islands, France is joined by most of its former black African colonies plus Equatorial Guinea, the former Belgian territories and some of the former Portuguese colonies in an annual Franco-African summit.

Not only does France maintain military bases in six independent African countries — Central African Republic, Comoro Islands (Mayotte), Djibouti, Gabon, Côte d'Ivoire, Senegal — plus Reunion, it has intervened with impunity all over the continent, including logistical support for Moroccan troops in Zaire during the first Shaba war in 1977 and direct intervention in 1978 (Shaba II), 1991 and 1993; and intervention in Gabon, Rwanda, Cote d'Ivoire, etc.[82] Until 1991, the 31st Brigade of the Zairian Armed Forces was trained and staffed by the French! In the last 25 years, there have been four major French military interventions in Chad: 1968-72, 1977-80, 1983-84, and since 1986. For France, Chad and other countries of Francophone Africa must remain its own *chasse gardee*.

That Africa is or ought to remain the neo-colonial preserve of the West and a major responsibility for West European countries in terms of the gendarme duty has been a major tenet of US foreign policy since 1960. President Ronald Reagan reaffirmed this position in 1983 as he sought to put pressure on the reluctant socialist regime of French President François Mitterand to intervene in the Chadian civil war. For its part, the United States has intervened, either directly or indirectly, in those situations where one of its European allies was incapable of or had failed to play a forceful role in the defence of Western interests. Zaire is the best example of this US role in Africa. There, the US replaced Belgium as the major arbiter of the country's destiny, but continues to deal with Zairian affairs within a multilateral strategy of imperialism in which Belgium and France are its key partners.[83] Elsewhere, the United States has replaced the former colonial powers as the major patron of the regimes governing most of the strategically important countries in the Mediterranean, northeast Africa and the Indian Ocean region, namely, Morocco, Tunisia, Egypt, Sudan, Somalia, and Kenya. In addition, it has established a naval base on the island of Diego Garcia in the Indian Ocean.

The reliance on foreign military assistance and support is a clear manifestation of the limitations of independence and, consequently, of the crisis of the state in Africa today. It is evident that, although the African states have the international system behind them with regard to their goals of territorial integrity and national sovereignty, they are for the most part still incapable of themselves developing viable internal security and external defence capabilities. At the same time, their continued dependence on the former colonial power and other world powers reflects not a situation in which African regimes are the puppets of these powers, but one in which there exits a compatibility of interests between them and their external allies and patrons.[84]

For the latter, support for African clients is often predicated on strategic and economic considerations. For the African clients, the primary motivation is political survival and all the advantages which go with it. It is to the preoccupation with power and wealth that I now turn for a further illumination of the nature of the state in post-colonial Africa.

Resource Extraction and Social Control

In addition to their security and defence preoccupations, African rulers strive to retain power as long as possible and to use it to advance their own material interests. Governmental activities in the area of nation-building and state capacity building are often pursued not as ends in themselves, i.e., as being indispensable to the entire process of national construction, but only in so far as they help to ensure the political survival and personal enrichment of those who control the state. The ideals of participation and democracy have been subordinated to the revenue, security and legitimation imperatives of the state, whose priority tasks consist of resource extraction and social control.[85]

In performing its global or political role as the factor of cohesion in society,[86] the state engages in three types of activity: the extraction of resources, the regulation of individual and social behaviour, and the distribution of goods and services. These activities are interdependent. Resource extraction is a *sine qua non* of all regulative and distributive activities. The state cannot perform these functions without the resources needed for carrying them out successfully. Its very organization and functioning is dependent on revenue or tax collection, taxes being "the source of life for the bureaucracy, the army . . . in short, for the whole apparatus of the executive power".[87] Likewise, the regulation of behaviour involves a recourse to legal and political sanctions with which the state may obtain public compliance with its extractive and distributive functions. As for the latter, which include the redistribution of resources for purposes of maintaining social harmony,[88] they enhance the state's legitimacy and consequently help to create a moral climate in which voluntary compliance with the state's extractive and regulative activities takes precedence over coercive means. Moreover, the state's distributive functions play a crucial role, even under capitalism, in the expansion of societal capacity or in the ability of the economy to produce more resources.[89]

Enhancing the state's capacity to fulfill these three functions adequately is a necessary condition for expanding its organization and effective presence in civil society, establishing a legitimate authority structure, and laying the groundwork for economic growth and development. As an authoritarian structure of control preoccupied with the political survival and the material interests of the ruling class, the post-colonial state is not radically different from its predecessor, the colonial state.

According to a Zairian historian, the ultimate significance of decolonization resides in "the setting-up of new states which are at the same time in rupture and in continuity with the colonial state, rupture with regard to state power, to the class holding the state, and continuity in the modes of existence and the functions of the state."[90] That is to say that the post-colonial state is for all intents and purposes a neo-colonial state, a politically independent structure within a basically unchanged economic framework. Thus, whether neo-colonial or revolutionary, conservative or progressive, the class in charge of the new state cannot be expected to implement a coherent development strategy on the basis of institutional structures that were meant to serve interests other than those of African workers and peasants.

Decolonization did not involve the necessary structural changes to the political economy to improve the chances for development. As an extension of the metropolitan state, the colonial state was a bourgeois type of state, but not a bourgeois democratic state as in Britain, France, Belgium and the Netherlands. It was an authoritarian state designed to fulfill the accumulation interests of metropolitan capital. With few exceptions, the post-colonial state has followed this path of capitalist development, in the interest of its own rulers and their metropolitan allies.

Given this reality, the neo-colonial state, like its colonial predecessor, is primarily concerned with the maintenance of law and order and the accumulation of wealth in the interest of its ruling class. Since the state is the major avenue of wealth accumulation as well as a source of wealth by virtue of its extensive control over economic resources, a major preoccupation of this class has been to expand and consolidate the state's role in the economy. Accordingly, the state is a major prize, the key object of intra-class fractional struggles. Power, and especially state power, is a zero-sum game, as being in or out has serious consequences for one's well-being as well as life itself. The emergence of patrimonial rulers as skilled arbitrators of the conflicting interests of various factions and groups is a necessary condition for establishing some form of effective rule under a neo-colonial state.

The state's role in the economy also brings the ruling class into sharp confrontation with the interests and aspirations of ordinary people. For the state's relationship to the popular classes revolves chiefly around the need to exercise effective social control over the latter. This is done or attempted through a variety of coercive and non-coercive means, including the activities of the state's economic management agencies. Rather than promoting development, the major goals of these agencies are resource extraction and social control. In the countryside, where the bulk of state revenue outside of the mineral sector is collected, agricultural production and marketing schemes are mainly subordinated to the requirements of revenue collection, the opportunities for personal enrichment associated with it, and the manifestation of the state's active presence and political control.[91]

The state is both a source of wealth and the means of defending it, domestically as well as internationally.[92] Domestically, the state's preoccupation with resource extraction, social control, and the personal enrichment of its officials has negative consequences for both development and democracy. For the neo-colonial state, a stable political order is one that is best captured by the slogan "one country, one leader". Relative stability requires that intra-elite conflicts be reduced to factional politics under the control and manipulation of the top leader. Opposition parties and free elections were not allowed because they represent real possibilities of political action by the masses, and it is precisely these possibilities that the neo-colonial state strives to suppress because the rulers of such states see democratic politics as destabilizing.

Free from public accountability and popular political control, African rulers have used the state to serve their own interests rather than those of society at large. With few exceptions, they have privatized the state itself. In this regard, the pertinent question with respect to the state's role in the economy is not a fateful dichotomy between more of less state involvement, as the ideologues of privatization would have it. It is rather the question of the nature of the state, or the interests it serves. In this context, state enterprises have failed not because they are state owned, but because of the manner in which they have been run as avenues of personal enrichment. As Claude Julien writes with respect to the public monopolies under the regime of Ferdinand Marcos in the Philippines, the parastatal sector of most Third World countries is in reality a "caricature of the public sector, in the service of truly private interests."[93]

It is this privatization of the state that constitutes the major obstacle to economic development. The mismanagement, corruption, capital flight and the other ills associated with it have not only crippled the economy in potentially rich countries like Nigeria and Zaire, but also reduced the state's ability to maintain the social infrastructure and thus serve the needs of ordinary people. The flight of capital perpetrated by national leaders has benefitted the developed Western countries in whose financial institutions the assets of the Third World have been deposited, devastating thereby their countries of origin.[94]

The amounts involved have been estimated to range between $4 and $6 billion by 1985 in the case of Zaire, or roughly more than the totality of the country's external debt of $4.5 billion in 1985.[95] For Nigeria, it is said to have represented about 42 percent of medium- and long-term external debt between 1976 and 1982.[96] The real figure is likely to be much higher, given the rapacity of the key figures in the Shagari regime whose plunder of the national treasury has had no equal in contemporary Africa. When the civilian regime came to power in 1979, they found a foreign reserves' surplus of $3 billion. By the time of their overthrow in December 1983, Nigeria had an external debt of over $20 billion!

The neo-colonial state itself constitutes an obstacle to development in Africa. As pointed out above, the deepening crisis of this state and its declining capacity for development has to be understood in a larger perspective as part of the general crisis of world capitalism. In addition to specifically domestic factors, the crisis of the post-colonial state is a function of the neo-colonial tasks that imperialism has assigned to it. These include the preservation of the country's position in the international division of labour as a source of raw materials and cheap labour, the internal creation and expansion of a lucrative domestic market for luxury goods, sophisticated technologies and turnkey investments unrelated to the absorptive capacity and the development needs of the economy, and the suppression of revolutionary ideas and movements likely to challenge this arrangement.

Given the absence of popular political control and other mechanisms of accountability, state officials work chiefly to advance their own careers and material interests rather than to carry out the duties associated with their agencies. The result is a growing incapacity on the part of the state to execute properly even routine duties such as the recording of vital statistics and socio-economic data.[97] Consequently, a salient aspect of the crisis of the post-colonial state in Africa is the fact of being characterized by the coexistence of absolute power and administrative decay, or by the dialectic of power and fragility.[98] Only timely support by external patrons and allies can be counted upon to prevent a total collapse of the central state machinery in those countries where administrative decay has seriously undermined the regime's hold on state power and its ability to govern the country.

Much of the external support for state capacity building in Africa and in other Third World countries goes to the military or security forces. It seems that raising the operational capacity of these forces is deemed more useful than developing the social services apparatus of the state since the former will provide the security needed by foreign investors to extract resources and to repatriate their profits from Africa.

In this context, it is important to stress the point that administrative decay is relative, not absolute, and that it seldom affects the entire state structure in a crippling manner. Thus, if the state is not doing so well with the delivery of social services, it is still alive and well through the active presence of its tax collectors, police, soldiers and other state officials in civil society, who not only extract resources legally and illegally from a somewhat helpless population, but also subject the latter to acts of harassment and repression. Likewise, if the security forces are basically a parade army and a paper tiger when it comes to waging war against armed opponents, as the Zairian armed forces proved in their disarray in the face of the *Front de Liberation National Congolais* (FLNC) forces in 1977 and 1978, they are still capable of killing unarmed civilians and of intimidating the majority of the population. In other words, a fragile military establishment is nonetheless a potent instrument of repression *vis-à-vis* the majority of citizens.

What is significant in terms of the crisis of the state is why organisations like the military are not capable of performing their official duties in a satisfactory manner. The lack of discipline, adequate training and operational efficacy on the part of Third World armies is generally a function of political factors, including the lack of a strong professional ethic on the part of the officer corps. Mahmoud Hussein points out in his analysis of Nasser's Egypt that a bourgeois type army loses its fighting ability when the behaviour of its officers is dominated by a "capitalist self-interest, the pursuit of private profit, and a taste for luxury and personal prestige".[99] In the advanced capitalist countries, such behavioural traits are tempered by a long and relatively uniform military tradition, and kept in check by enforceable regulations as well as by civilian control over the military.

Generally, African military officers are not secure about their career opportunities, and they operate in a political environment full of intrigue. They are consequently uncertain of the future and seek therefore to acquire wealth and to enjoy life while they can. Their preoccupation with wealth, luxury and pleasure has a detrimental effect on military leadership, training and discipline. What is true for the military is even more so for other organs of the state system, including the judiciary. For most high-level officials, the state is a structure of control to be used for the pursuit of private interests. The most important of these is personal enrichment, a goal made easier to attain because of the state's extensive involvement in the economy.

Finally, the African state cannot hope to rely exclusively on coercion as a means of social control. Like states everywhere, it has attempted to resolve its crisis of legitimacy through recourse to political indoctrination. The ideological spectrum has included ideas and doctrines like African Socialism, authenticity, and Marxism-Leninism.[100] On the whole, these ideologies have been presented in a way that suggests a close affinity, if not identity, between the aspirations of the masses and the actual goals and politics of the state. In reality, however, the state bourgeoisie subverts through concrete practice the very meaning of ideas whose realization would undermine its own interests. Generally, these ideologies mask the contradictions of post-colonial Africa, where most people continue to live in poverty while the ruling minority is elevated to the ranks of the world's wealthiest groups.

Conclusion

Nation-building and state building are part of the struggle of the African people for liberation and development. They cannot be understood in isolation, as they are related to, and shaped by, the class contradictions of the process of national liberation.

All over the continent, the anti-colonial struggle was a great event in the lives of the African people. Both the masses and their *petit-bourgeois* nationalist leaders expected a lot from it. The masses had hoped that their living conditions would improve as a result of what they saw as a revolutionary experience, and this was in fact what their leaders promised them. But the promise was not honoured after independence, for many reasons, one of which was the fact that the anti-colonial struggle had masked the class contradictions between the *petit-bourgeoisie* and ordinary people. These contradictions became manifest after independence when, instead of fulfilling their promises, the new rulers responded to the people's demands either with more promises or with repression.

The present crisis of the post-colonial state can be traced to this breakdown of the popular alliance formed during the independence struggle. Preoccupied with their own political survival and material interests, African rulers have for the most part failed to satisfy their people's expectations of independence. The post-colonial state serves principally the interests of those who control it as well as those of their external allies and patrons. The struggle must go on, and it must involve the transformation of the state so that it can serve the interests of African workers and peasants.

Such a radical restructuring of the neo-colonial state and society is precisely what the masses have placed on the agenda in their determination to realize genuine liberation and development. The "second independence" movement in countries like Zaire, Chad and Uganda, the heroic liberation struggle in Southern Africa, the struggles for national self-determination in northeast Africa and Western Sahara, and the fight for democratic rights from the Cape to Cairo are well related to the continuing process of liberation from imperialism, colonialism and neo-colonialism. Their success will depend not only on the balance of social forces worldwide, but also on the ability of these movements to recruit and retain within their organizations, a dedicated body of revolutionary intellectuals capable of providing the people with the necessary tools to build a better society.

This is the essential message of Amilcar Cabral and his revolutionary legacy for Africa. It is a legacy that is part and parcel of both historical materialism as a universal science of society and history and the Western intellectual tradition from which it emerged. This is a tradition in which philosophers from the time of Socrates to the present have emphasized the social responsibility of intellectuals. It is, in other words, part of the universal tradition of social criticism by intellectuals. But criticism of the *status quo* is not to be made for the sake of criticism and within the relative comfort of academia. It is a weapon whose value is realized only when it is added to the arsenal of the struggling masses in search of a better life for themselves and a secure future for their children. *A luta continua!*

Footnotes

1. On the theory of the capitalist state, see Nicos Poulantzas, *Political Power and Social Classes* (New Left Books, London, 1973).

2. That political communities based on such a relationship did exist in the pre-modern era seems to be well-established. Europe did not invent orderly political communities.

3. C. Northcote Parkinson, *The Evolution of Political Thought* (Houghton Mifflin Co., Boston, 1958), p. 7.

4. *Ibid.,* p. 168.

5. Thomas Hodgkin, "The Relevance of 'Western' Ideas for the New African States," in T. Rowland Pennock (ed.) *Self-Government in Modernizing Nations* (Prentice-Hall, Englewood Cliffs, NJ, 1964).

6. Rupert Emerson, *From Empire to Nation: The Rise to Self-Assertion of Asian and African Peoples* (Beacon Press, Boston, 1962), p. 53.

7. Hodgkin, "The Relevance of 'Western' Ideas," p.60.

8. V. I. Lenin, "The Three Sources and Three Component Parts of Marxism," in Lenin, *Selected Works*, Vol. 1 (Progress Publishers, Moscow, 1977), pp. 44-48. See also August H. Nimtz, Jr., "Marxism," in *The Oxford Companion to Politics of the World*, edited by Joel Krieger (Oxford University Press, New York, 1993), pp. 569-575.

9. G. David Garson, "From Policy Science to Policy Analysis: A Quarter Century of Progress," in William N. Dunn (ed.) *Policy Analysis: Perspectives, Concepts, and Methods* (JAI Press, Greenwich, CT, 1986), pp. 3-22.

10. *Ibid,* p. 20.

11. Much of the following survey of Western political thought is based on my outline for the introductory course in political science at the National University of Zaire (1971-73), published as *Introduction à la science politique* (Editions du Mont Noir, Lubumbashi, 1972), pp. 18-27.

12. A.R.M. Murray, *An Introduction to Political Philosophy* (Cohen and West, London, 1953), p. 55.

13. See Seymour Martin Lipset, *Political Man: The Social Bases of Politics* (Doubleday and Co., New York, 1960).

14. George S. Sabine and Thomas L. Thorson, *A History of Political Theory,* 4th ed. (Dryden Press, Hinsdale, 1973), p. 329.

15. Murray, *Introduction to Political Philosophy,* p. 85.

16. Eric Rouleau, "Guerre et intoxication au Chad," *Le Monde Diplomatique,* September 1983.

17. Antonio Gramsci, *Selections from the Prison Notebooks* (International Publishers, New York, 1971), p. 142 shows the contrast in this regard between Bodin and Machiavelli.

18. Maurice Duverger, *Sociologie politique* (Presses Universitaires de France, Paris, 1968), p.3.

19. Martin Carnoy, *The State and Political Theory* (Princeton University Press, Princeton, 1984), pp. 19-21.

20. Parkinson, *The Evolution of Political Thought,* p. 311.

21. Rousseau, *On the Social Contract,* cited in *ibid,* pp. 205 and 311.

22. Barrington Moore, Jr., *Social Origins of Dictatorship and Democracy* (Beacon Press, Boston, 1966), p. 523.

23. Alvin W. Gouldner, *The Coming Crisis of Western Sociology* (Heinemann, London, 1970), p. 447.

24. For an excellent critique of modernization theory with respect to nation-building see Donal B. Cruise O'Brien, "Modernization, Order and the Erosion of a Democratic Ideal: American Political Science 1960-70," *Journal of Development Studies,* vol. 8, No. 4, 1972, pp. 351-378.

25. Nzongola-Ntalaja, *Revolution and Counter-Revolution in Africa* (Zed Books and IFAA, London, 1987).

26. Reinhard Bendix, *Nation-Building and Citizenship* (John Wiley & Sons, New York, 1964), p. 18. A major theorist of nation-building in the historicist tradition of Max Weber and the modernization school, Bendix summarizes the main tenets of his historical sociology in *Force, Fate and Freedom* (University of California Press, Berkeley, 1984).

27. Clifford Geertz, "The Integrative Revolution: Primordial Sentiments and Civil Politics in the New States," in Clifford Geertz (ed.), *Old Societies and New States* (Free Press, New York, 1963).

28. Apter's major theoretical work in this respect is *The Politics of Modernization* (University of Chicago Press, Chicago, 1965). Zolberg's major statement on the subject is his article entitled "The Structure of Political Conflict in the New States of Tropical Africa," *American Political Science Review,* Vol. 62, No. 1, March 1968, pp. 70-87.

29. David E. Apter, *Ghana in Transition* (Atheneum, New York, 1963), pp. 80-81; Apter, *The Political Kingdom in Uganda* (Princeton University Press, Princeton, 1961, 1967), pp. 18-20.

30. Zolberg, "The Structure of Political Conflict," pp. 73-74.

31. Samuel P. Huntington, "Political Development and Political Decay," *World Politics*, vol. 17, no. 3, 1965, pp. 399-402.

32. Aristide R. Zolberg, *Creating Political Order: The Party-States of West Africa* (Rand McNally, Chicago, 1966).

33. See Goran Hyden, *Beyond Ujamaa in Tanzania: Underdevelopment and an Uncaptured Peasantry*, (University of California Press, Berkeley, 1980), his *No Shortcuts to Progress: African Development Management in Perspective,* (University of California Press, Berkeley, 1983), and his "African Social Structure and Economic Development", in Robert J. Berg and Jennifer Seymour Whitaker (eds.) *Strategies for African Development* (University of California Press, Berkeley, 1986), pp. 52-80.

34. Hyden, "African Social Structure," p. 58.

35. This critique of Hyden's position is part of my "Governance and Economic Management: Historical, Social and Institutional Issues," paper presented at the 2nd session of the Committee on African Development Strategies (A Joint Project of the Council on Foreign Relations and the Overseas Development Council), Washington, D.C., 23 October 1984.

36. On the question of whether Africa should be analyzed as a special case, with its own theories and concepts, Amilcar Cabral replied that we "should not forget that whatever the particularities of the African case and the possible originality of African societies, the laws of their development are the same as those of all other human societies." Amilcar Cabral, *Unite et lutte*, Vol. 1: *L'arme de la théorie* (Maspero, Paris, 1975), p. 273.

37. J. V. Stalin, *Works*, vol. 2 (Foreign Languages Publishing House, Moscow, 1953), p. 307, emphasis in original. Stalin wrote *Marxism and the National Question* between November 1912 and January 1913 in Vienna.

38. Linda Burnham and Bob Wing, "Toward a Communist Analysis of Black Oppression and Black Liberation," Part I: "Critique of the Black Nation Thesis," *Line of March*, No. 7, 1981, p. 40.

39. *Ibid.,* p. 41.

40. See Nicos Poulantzas, *L'Etat, le pouvoir, le socialisme* (Presses Universitaires de France, Paris, 1978), pp. 102-133, English trans. *State, Power, Socialism* (New Left Books, London, 1980); Samir Amin, *The Arab Nation* (Zed Press, London, 1978).

41. Poulantzas, *L'Etat, le pouvoir, le socialisme*, pp. 105-106, emphasis in the original.

42. Samir Amin, *Unequal Development: An Essay on the Social Formations of Peripheral Capitalism* (Monthly Review Press, New York, 1976), p. 29.

43. Samir Amin, *Class and Nation* (Monthly Review Press, New York, 1980).

44. *Ibid.,* p. 20.

45. *Ibid*, p. 42.

46. Amin, *The Arab Nation*, p. 10.

47. *Ibid*, p. 11.

48. Poulantzas, *L'Etat, le pouvoir, le socialisme*, p. 124.

49. *Ibid*, pp. 110-127.

50. Amin, *The Arab Nation*, p. 81.

51. The Kuba people of Zaire are a particularly good example of the pre-colonial nation. In his authoritative history of the Kuba peoples *The Children of Woot* (University of Wisconsin Press, Madison, 1978), Jan Vansina presents them as a multi-ethnic society consisting of five ethnic groups. From his analysis, it can be shown that the Kuba Kingdom consisted of one nation — a Kuba nation — relying heavily for its identity on the central Kuba chiefdoms led by the Bushoong as its core group and supported at different levels of attachment by the peripheral Kuba chiefdoms, which shared a common culture with the core group, and by four ethnic minorities (Kete, Coofa, Cwa, Mbeengi), which were for the most part oppressed minorities (see p. 166).

52. For a brief history of these states, see David Birmingham, *Central Africa to 1970: Zambezia, Zaire and the South Atlantic*, Chapters from the Cambridge History of Africa (Cambridge University Press, Cambridge, 1981).

53. Nzongola-Ntalaja, "Les chefs tradionnels dans l'administration locale coloniale au Dahomey et en Sierra Leone" *Cahiers Zairois d'Etudes Politiques et Sociales*, No. 1, April 1973, pp. 95-116.

54. Jean Suret-Canale, *Afrique noire accidentale et centrale*, vol. 2: L'ère coloniale (1900-1945) (Editions Sociales, Paris 1964), defines colonialism as a system of economic exploitation, political and administrative oppression, and cultural oppression.

55. A good example of how the influence of Garveyism went beyond English-speaking Africa is its penetration of the Belgian Congo, where the colonialists had tried their best to shield the country from the winds of change. See Muzong Kodi, "Garveyism and Kimbanguism: Belgian Reactions to a Messianic Movement in the Congo", *The Panafricanist*, no. 3, 1971, pp. 1-8, and Wyatt Mac Gaffrey, *Modern Kongo Prophets: Religion in a Plural Society* (Indiana University Press, Bloomington, 1983), p. 7.

56. Obafemi Awolowo, *Path to Nigerian Freedom* (Faber, London, 1947). This thesis was further developed in most of Chief Awolowo's later publications.

57. Kwame Nkrumah, *Africa Must Unite* (Heinemann, London, 1963).

58. Amilcar Cabral, *Revolution in Guinea: Selected Texts* (Monthly Review Press, New York, 1972), p. 71.,

59. Walter Rodney, "Toward the Sixth Pan-African Congress: Aspects of the International Class Struggle in Africa, the Caribbean and America", in Horace Campbell (ed.) *Pan-Africanism: The Struggle Against Imperialism and Neocolonialism* (Afro-Carib Publications, Toronto, 1975), p. 21.

60. Crawford Young, "Patterns of Social Conflict: State, Class, and Ethnicity", *Daedalus*, vol. 111, no. 2, 1982, pp. 80-81.

61. On the year 1956 as a crucial date for the liberation and international working class movements, see Yes Benot, "Amilcar Cabral and the International Working Class Movement", *Latin American Perspectives* 41, vol. 11, no. 2, 1984, p. 82.

62. See John Macrum, *The Angolan Revolution*, vol. 1 (MIT Press, Cambridge, 1969), pp. 49-100, for a history of Kongo nationalism in Angola.

63. Like the *petit-bourgeoisie*, they were subject to the integrative mechanisms of an inter-ethnic urban or semi-urban milieu: living and working together, speaking the same *lingua franca* of the territory or the region, and developing a common culture in lifestyle, popular music and entertainment.

64. According to Tony Hodges, *Western Sahara: The Roots of a Desert War* (Lawrence Hill & Co., Westport, CT, 1983), pp. 149-150, the Saharawi people of Western Sahara never formed a nation in pre-colonial times and were more conscious of their tribal or clan identity than of any notion of supra-tribal or national identity. "Nevertheless," Hodges writes, "as men of the desert, great camel-herding nomads and speakers of the Hassaniya dialect of Arabic, the Saharawis did, in a broad cultural sense, regard themselves as a very different people from the predominantly Tashelhit-speaking sedentary or semi nomadic Berbers to the immediate north."

65. Crawford Young, *The Politics of Cultural Pluralism*, (University of Wisconsin Press, Madison, 1976), p. 93.

66. Parkinson, *The Evolution of Political Thought*, p. 310.

67. Amilcar Cabral, *Unity and Struggle: Speeches and Writings* (Monthly Review Press, New York, 1979, p. 241.

68. J.F. Adde Ajayi, "Expectations of Independence," *Daedalus*, Vol. 111, No. 2, 1982, p. 5.

69. *Ibid,* pp. 5-6.

70. The best statement of this misconception is by Gary D. Ness, *Bureaucracy and Rural Development in Malaysia* (University of California Press, Berkeley, 1967), for whom new states, modernization and development administration are functionally interrelated phenomena.

71. Dudley Seers, "The Meaning of Development", in Norman T. Uphoff and Warren F. Ilchman (eds.), *The Political Economy of Development* (University of California Press, Berkeley, 1972), pp. 123-129.

72. For an excellent study of the state and civil society in Tanzania, see Issa G. Shivji (ed.) *The State and the Working People in Tanzania* (CODESRIA, Dakar, 1985).

73. Crawford Young "Africa's Colonial Legacy", in Robert J. Berg and Jennifer Seymour Whitaker (eds.), *Strategies for African Development* (University of California Press, Berkeley, 1986), pp. 26 and 40.

74. For more on the role of the military in African politics, see Peter Anyang' Nyong'o, "Military Intervention in African Politics", *Third World Affairs 1986*, pp. 171-179.

75. Nzongola-Ntalaja and Laura Bigman, "The Arms Race and the Process of National Construction in Developing Countries", *UNESCO Yearbook on Peace and Conflict Studies*, Vol. VIII, 1987.

76. See Young, *The Politics of Cultural Pluralism*, pp. 474-489, for a brief history of Bengali nationalism and the birth of Bangladesh.

77. So far, the most useful publications on the Chadian civil war have been in French: Robert Buijtenhuijs, *Le Frolinat et les révoltes populaires du Tchad, 1965-1976* (Mouton, The Hague, 1978); Pierre Bell, "Le coup d'Etat militaire au Tchad", *Le Monde Diplomatique*, May 1975; Didier Baussy, "Le Tchad, pays divisé: une 'indépendance' qui se conquiert'', *Le Monde Diplomatique*, May 1976; Thierry Michalon, "Le drame du Tchad et

l'héritage colonial de l'Afrique: l'échec de la greffe jacobine", *Le Monde Diplomatique*, April 1979; Agnès Thivent, "L'impossible mission de l'armée française", *Le Monde Diplomatique*, March 1980; Guy Labertit, "Tchad: Une paix fragile pour un peuple trompé", in *ibid.*; Thierry Michalon, "L'impuissance d'un Etat fictif", *Le Monde Diplomatique*, September 1983; Eric Rouleau, "Guerre et intoxication au Tchad", in *ibid.*; Gérard Galtier, "Culture arabe et culture africaine: comment reconstruire l'Etat tchadien", *Le Monde Diplomatique*, November 1984; Paul-Marie de la Gorce, "Risques accrus d'interventions étrangères au Tchad", *Le Monde Diplomatique*, February 1987; Alain Gresh, "Les visées et les craintes du régime libyen", in *ibid.* But see also Virginia Thompson and Richard Adloff, *Conflict in Chad* (Institute of International Studies, University of California, Berkeley, 1981).

78.   For a background to the Sudanese conflict, see chapters by Bona Malwal and Roland Marchal in Georges Nzongola-Ntalaja (ed.) *Conflict in the Horn of Africa* (African Studies Association Press, Atlanta, 1991), pp. 117-147.

79.   See Guy Martin, "The Franc Zone, Underdevelopment and Dependency in Francophone Africa", *Third World Quarterly*, vol. 8, no. 1, 1986, pp. 205-235. On the Lome Convention and multilateral imperialism, see D. Wadada Nabudere, *Essays on the Theory and Practice of Imperialism* (Onyx Press, London, and Tanzania Publishing House, Dar es Salaam, 1979) ch. 5; Guy Martin, "African-European Economic Relations under the Lome Convention: Commodities and the Scheme of Stabilization of Export Earnings", *African Studies Review*, vol. 27, no. 3, 1984, pp. 41-66.

80.   See Amilcar Cabral, "Portugal is not an Imperialist Country", in Aquino de Braganca and Immanuel Wallerstein (eds.) *The African Liberation Reader, Vol. 1: The Anatomy of Colonialism* (Zed Books, London, 1982), pp. 31-34; Perry Anderson, "Portugal and the End of Ultra-Colonialism", *New Left Review*, 1962, no. 15, pp. 83-102; no. 16, pp. 88-123; and no. 17, pp. 85-114.

81.   There is an abundant literature on French neo-colonialism and militarism in Africa. On the former, see among other sources: Edward Bustin, "The Limits of French Intervention in Africa: A Study in Applied Neo-colonialism", Boston University African Studies Centre Working Papers, no. 54, 1982; Richard Joseph, "The Gaullist Legacy: Patterns of French Neo-colonialism", *Review of African Political Economy*, no. 6, 1976, pp. 4-13; Guy Martin, "Bases of France's African Policy", *Journal of Modern African Studies*, vol. 23, no. 2, 1985, pp. 189-208.

82.   For more information on French military intervention in Africa, see Julian Crandall Hollick, "French Intervention in Africa in 1978", *The World Today*, February 1979, pp. 71-80; Robin Luckham, "French Militarism in Africa", *Review of African Political Economy*, no. 24, 1982, pp. 55-84.

83.   The Senegalese scholar and opposition leader, Abdoulaye Bathily, sees a similar process emerging in his own country,"a gradual process of a country being transformed from a preserve of French neo-colonialism into a multi-colony under the leadership of the United States." See his 'Senegal's Fraudulent "Democratic Opening"' in *Institute for African Alternatives, Africa's Crisis* (IFAA, London, 1987), p. 88.

84.   I have already developed this argument in my *Class Struggles and National Liberation in Africa* (Omenana, Roxbury, MA, 1982), pp. 91-95.

85. For a fuller discussion of each of these imperatives, see Young "Africa's Colonial Legacy", pp. 38-45.
86. Poulantzas, *Political Power and Social Classes*, p. 51.
87. Karl Marx, *The Eighteenth Brumaire of Louis Bonaparte* (International Publishers, New York, 1963), p. 128.
88. James O'Connor, *The Fiscal Crisis of the State* (St. Martin's Press, New York, 1973), P. 7.
89. *Ibid.*, pp. 6-7.
90. Elikia M'Bokolo, "Historicité et pouvoir d'Etat en Afrique noire", *Relations Internationales*, no. 324, 1983, pp. 197-213.
91. See Keith Hart, *The Political Economy of West African Agriculture* (Cambridge University Press, Cambridge, 1982).
92. Christopher Clapham, *Third World Politics: An Introduction* (University of Wisconsin Press, Madison, 1985), p. 40.
93. Claude Julien, "La démocratie et l'argent", *Le Monde Diplomatique*, April 1986, p. 6.
94. *Ibid*, p. 1.
95. Jean Coussy and Philippe Hugon, "Trois pays, trois types de constrainte", *Le Monde Diplomatique*, April 1986, p. 17.
96. *Ibid*, p. 17.
97. See Nzongola-Ntalaja, "Urban Administration in Zaire: A Study of Kananga, 1971-73", Unpublished Ph.D. dissertation, University of Wisconsin-Madison, 1975, for a detailed analysis of the performance of routine administrative duties in Zaire.
98. Clapham, *Third World Politics*, pp. 39-44.
99. Mahmoud Hussein, *Class Conflict in Egypt,* 1945-1971 (Monthly Review Press, New York, 1973), p. 257, note 8. See also Jack Woddis, *New Theories of Revolution* (International Publishers, New York, 1972), p. 234, for a similar case from Latin America, that of Batista's army in Cuba.
100. Studies of these ideologies include Young, *Ideology and Development*; David and Marina Ottaway, *Afrocommunism* (Africana Publishing Co., New York, 1981); John Saul, "Ideology in Africa: Decomposition and Recomposition" in Gwendolen M. Carter and Patrick O'Meara (eds.) *African Independence: The First Twenty-Five Years* (Indiana University Press, Bloomington, 1985), pp. 301-329; Ali A. Mazrui, "Africa Between Ideology and Technology: Two Frustrated Forces of Change", in *ibid.*, pp. 274-300; N. Tutashinda, "Les mystifications de l'authenticité", *La Pensée*, no. 175, 1974, pp. 68-81; Nzongola-Ntalaja, "The Authenticity of Neocolonialism: Ideology and Class Struggle in Zaire", *Berkeley Journal of Sociology*, vol. XXII, 1977-78, pp. 115-130.

Southern Africa Political Economy Series

SAPES Trust

The Southern Africa Political Economy Series (SAPES) Trust is a not-for-profit organisation whose main objectives are to promote and nurture social science research, debate, teaching and publications in Southern Africa. Its programmes, which operate on a network concept, are built around the major theme of *Problems and Prospects for Regional Political and Economic Cooperation in Southern Africa;* and seek to relate academic research to policy issues and public concerns in the region. Among its multiple fora, SAPES Trust publishes a monthly research journal, the *Southern Africa Political and Economic Monthly (SAPEM)*, the only journal of its kind on the continent. SAPES Trust research results are also disseminated through the monograph, occasional and seminar series, in addition to the *SAPES Book Series.* The former series is based on papers presented by visiting and guest scholars at the *Southern Africa Regional Institute for Policy Studies (SARIPS)* — a division of the SAPES Trust. In particular, the occasional paper series is designed to project conceptual and theoretical issues that might also constitute research themes for the SARIPS. The subjects covered are those that are pertinent or relate to the historical, political and economic process in Southern Africa. The SAPES Trust's Central Secretariat is located at 4 Deary Avenue, Belgravia, Harare, Zimbabwe.

About the Author

Georges Nzongola-Ntalaja is the Deputy President of the African Association of Political Science and Professor of African Studies at Howard University.

ISBN 1-77905-012-7